BOLT
BOOKS™

All Charged Up
A Look at Electricity

Jennifer Boothroyd

Lerner Publications Company
Minneapolis

To Girl Scout troop 10067, whose energy is quite shocking!

Lerner Publications Company
A division of Lerner Publishing Group, Inc.
241 First Avenue North
Minneapolis, MN 55401 U.S.A.

Website address: www.lernerbooks.com

Library of Congress Cataloging-in-Publication Data

Boothroyd, Jennifer, 1972–
　　All charged up : a look at electricity / by Jennifer Boothroyd.
　　　　p.　　cm. — (Lightning bolt books™—Exploring physical science)
　　Includes index.
　　ISBN 978-0-7613-6094-0 (lib. bdg. : alk. paper)
　　1. Electricity—Juvenile literature.　I. Title.
　　QC527.2.B665 2011
　　537—dc22　　　　　　　　　　　　　　　　　2010027981

Manufactured in the United States of America
1 — CG — 12/31/10

Contents

What Is Electricity?

Electricity is a form of energy. Many people depend on electricity.

Electricity brings light to the library so that this girl can read.

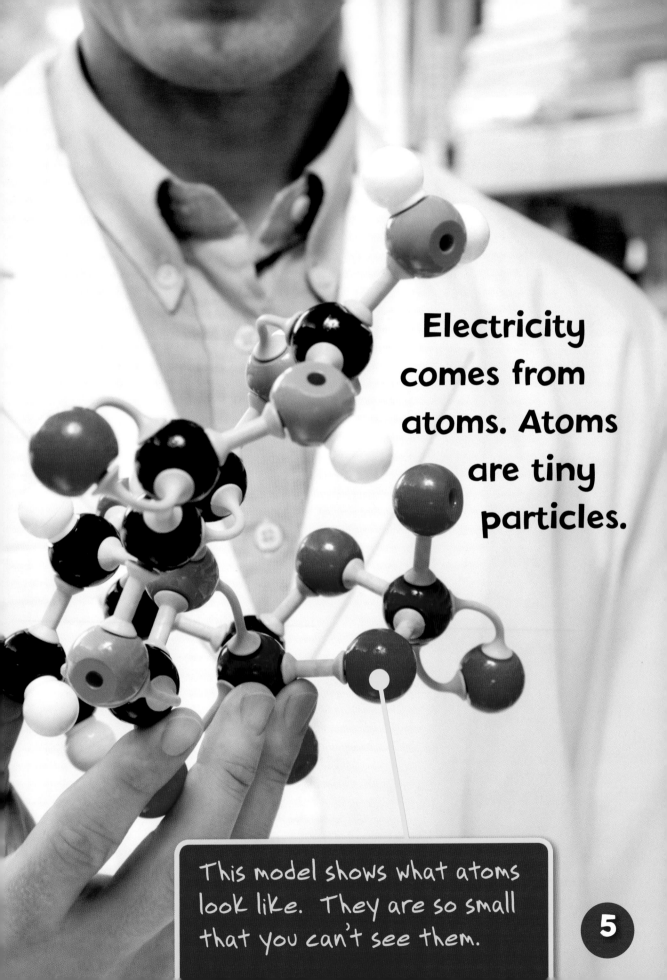

Electricity comes from atoms. Atoms are tiny particles.

This model shows what atoms look like. They are so small that you can't see them.

Everything on Earth is made of atoms. Books, desks, air, and even you are made of atoms!

Atoms have three parts. Protons and neutrons are in the center. Electrons circle around the center.

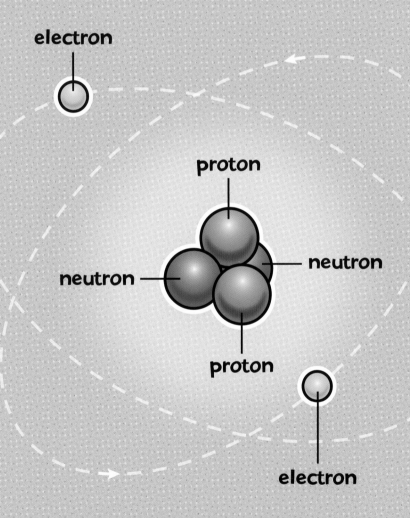

electron

proton

neutron — neutron

neutron

proton

electron

The Parts of an Atom

Electrons moving between atoms make electricity.

Electricity is created when electrons travel from one atom to another.

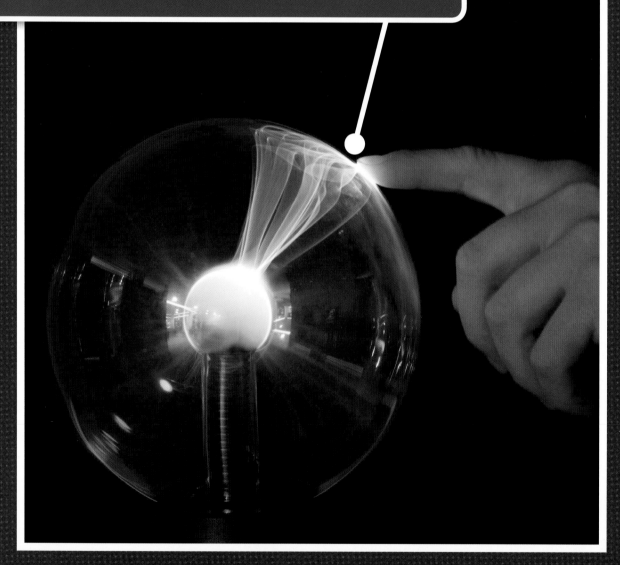

Static Electricity

Static electricity is made when two objects rub together. You can see and feel static electricity. It makes your hair stand up.

Has your hair ever stood on end after you combed it? The comb rubbing against your hair makes electrons move between atoms.

Static electricity can make sparks. Some sparks are tiny.

You may see tiny sparks when a sweater rubs against you as you put it on.

Other sparks are huge.
Lightning is a huge spark of
static electricity.

Lightning is made
when ice crystals
rub together inside
a cloud.

Current Electricity

Static electricity lasts for only a short time.

When a comb stops rubbing on your hair, electrons stop moving between atoms. Your hair will soon lie flat.

Electricity lasts longer when there's a steady flow of electrons. A steady flow of electrons is called an electric current.

An electric current makes this lantern glow.

An electric current flows through a conductor. A conductor is any material that lets electrons move from atom to atom. Copper is a great conductor.

Copper wires do a good job of carrying electric current.

Wood and rubber are not good conductors. Electricity does not move through them easily.

The soles of sneakers are made of rubber. Electricity does not travel well through rubber.

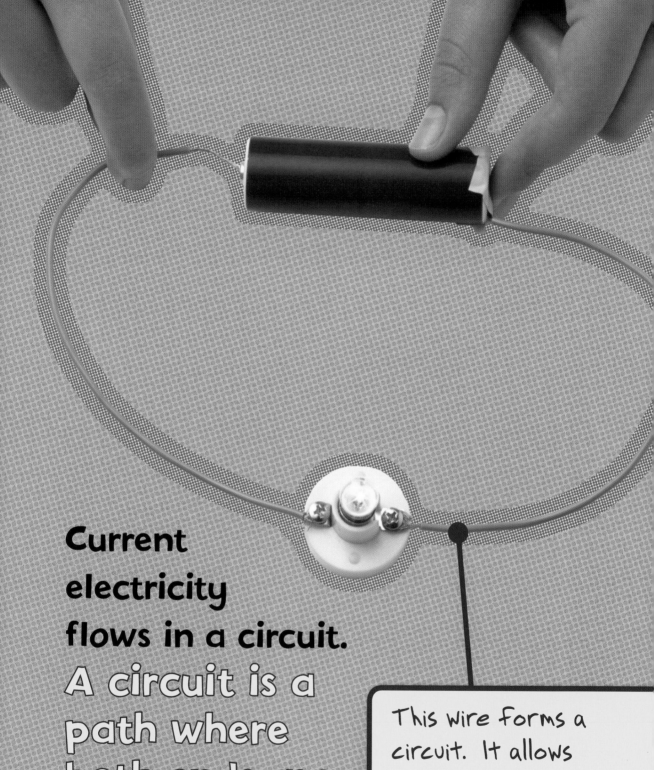

Current electricity flows in a circuit. A circuit is a path where both ends are connected.

This wire forms a circuit. It allows the current of electricity to light up the lightbulb.

A switch can stop and start the flow of electricity. Flip the switch to turn on the lights. Push the power button to turn off the TV.

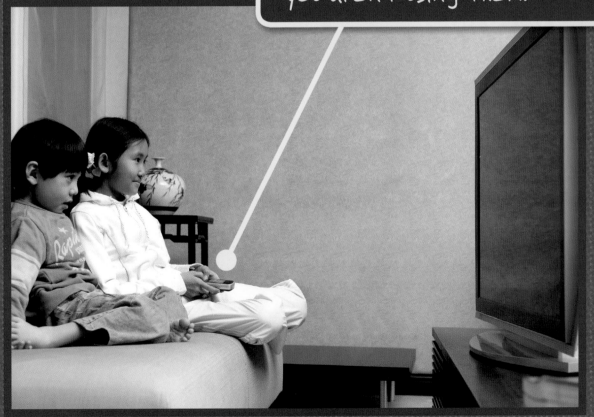

Use electricity wisely. Turn off TVs and lights when you aren't using them.

Sources of Electricity

Current electricity is created at power plants. Power plants are factories that make electricity.

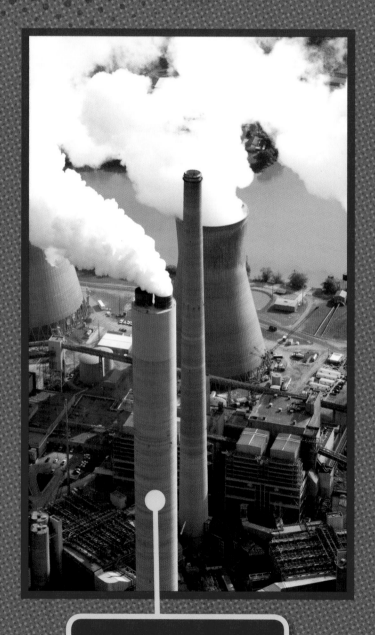

This is a power plant.

Some power plants use water to make electricity. Others burn coal. Still others use energy from the sun or the wind.

Machines called turbines turn wind energy into electricity.

The electricity from power plants travels through wires. The wires carry electricity into buildings. People plug power cords into outlets to use the electricity.

Power wires such as these carry electricity into homes.

Batteries are also sources of electricity.

Batteries store electricity. They let people use electricity without wires from a power plant.

Cars have a large battery. The electricity from the battery helps cars start.

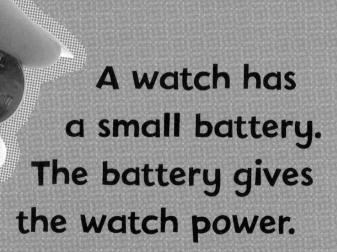

A watch has a small battery. The battery gives the watch power.

People must be careful with electricity. Electricity can burn your skin. It can cause a fire.

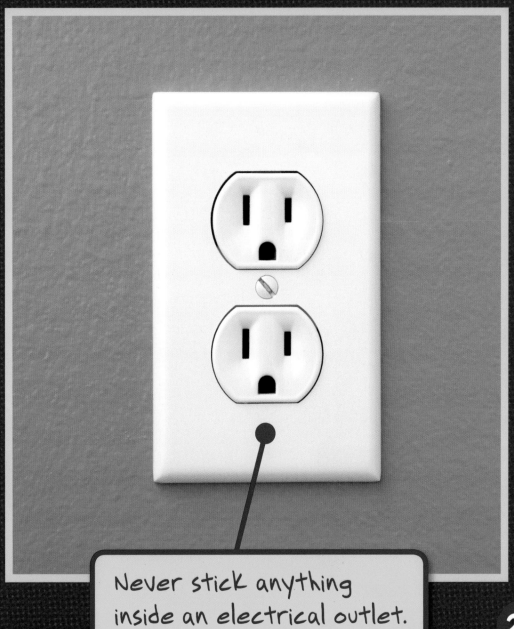

Never stick anything inside an electrical outlet.

Uses for Electricity

Many people use electricity every day. Electricity can make heat.

The heat from an electric stove cooks food.

Electricity can make light and sound.

Electricity powers the equipment that lets you watch a movie.

Electricity can put things into motion.

Electricity helps these clothes dryers run.

Electricity is an important part of our lives.

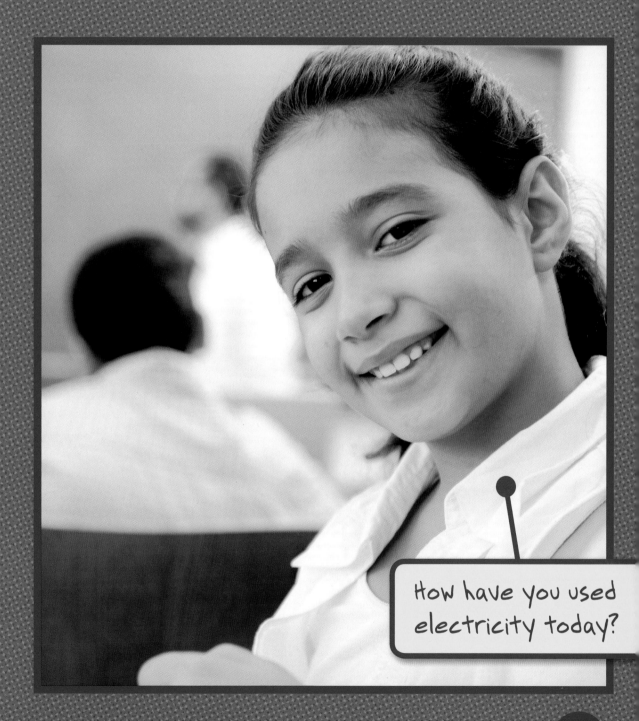

How have you used electricity today?

Activity
Static Sorter

Static electricity can be used to sort tiny objects quickly. Try this activity to see how it works.

What you need:

a **pinch** of **sugar**

a **pinch** of **black pepper**

a **plastic comb**

a **piece** of **wool fabric**

What you do:

1. Make a small pile of sugar and pepper on a counter. The sugar and pepper should be mixed together.

2. Rub the comb with the wool fabric very quickly for thirty seconds. The comb is now charged with static electricity.

3. Hold the comb a few inches over the pile. Slowly lower the comb over the pile.

4. Stop when the pepper starts sticking to the comb. The pepper sticks first because it is lighter than the sugar.

Glossary

atom: a tiny particle. Everything on Earth is made of atoms.

circuit: a path where both ends are connected

conductor: any material that allows electrons to keep moving from atom to atom

electric current: a steady flow of electrons between atoms

electron: one of the three parts of an atom. Electrons circle around an atom's center.

neutron: one of the three parts of an atom. Neutrons are in the center of an atom.

power plant: a large factory that makes electricity

proton: one of the three parts of an atom. Protons are in the center of an atom.

static electricity: a kind of electricity made when two objects rub together

Further Reading

The Bakken Museum
http://www.thebakken.org

BBC Schools Science Clips:
Using Electricity
http://www.bbc.co.uk/schools/
scienceclips/ages/6_7/electricity.shtml

Frankenstein's Lightning Laboratory
http://www.miamisci.org/af/sln/frankenstein/
safety.html

Schuh, Mari C. *Electricity*. Minneapolis: Bellwether Media, 2008.

Walker, Sally M. *Electricity*. Minneapolis: Lerner Publications Company, 2006.

Waring, Geoff. *Oscar and the Bird: A Book about Electricity*. Cambridge, MA: Candlewick Press, 2009.

Index

Photo Acknowledgments

The images in this book are used with the permission of: © Ronen/Shutterstock Images, p. 2; © Dave& Les Jacobs/Blend Images/Getty Images, p. 4; © Glow Wellness/ SuperStock, p. 5; © Monkey Business Images/Dreamstime.com, p. 6; © Laura Westlund/ Independent Picture Service, p. 7; © Heinrich van den Berg/Gallo Images/Getty Images, p. 8; © iStockphoto.com/Heidi Anglesey, p. 9; © Laurence Monneret/The Image Bank/Getty Images, p. 10; © iStockphoto.com/Paul Lampard, p. 11; © Andersson, Staffan/Johner Images/Getty Images, p. 12; © Radius Images/Photolibrary, p. 13; © iStockphoto.com/syagci, p. 14; © iStockphoto.com/Spencer Sternberg, p. 15; © Dave King/Dorling Kindersley/Getty Images, p. 16; © Corbis/Photolibrary, p. 17; © Harrison Shull/Aurora/Getty Images, p. 18; © Jon Boyes/Photographer's Choice RF/Getty Images, p. 19; © Ted Foxx/Alamy, p. 20; © Karyn R. Millet/Workbook Stock/Getty Images, p. 21; © iStockphoto.com/hywit dimyadl, p. 22 (top); © David Good/Shutterstock Images, p. 22 (bottom); © iStockphoto.com/Patrick Herrera, p. 23; © Photoboxer/Dreamstime.com, p. 24; © Stockbyte/Getty Images, p. 25; © Caroline Schiff/Blend Images/Getty Images, p. 26; © Zurijeta/Shutterstock Images, p. 27; © Tyler Boyes/Shutterstock Images, p. 28 (wool scarf); © justin maresch/Shutterstock Images, p. 28 (black pepper); © EuToch/ Shutterstock Images, p. 28 (blue comb); © Jzzzzs/Dreamstime.com, p. 28 (sugar); © 350jb | Dreamstime.com, p. 30; © carroteater | Dreamstime.com, p. 31.

Front cover: © David R. Frazier Photolibrary Inc./Alamy.